A DREAM FROM GOD

and a collection of poetry

MARGE KEATON

authorHOUSE

AuthorHouse™
1663 Liberty Drive
Bloomington, IN 47403
www.authorhouse.com
Phone: 833-262-8899

Published by AuthorHouse 10/25/2024

ISBN: 979-8-8230-3077-9 (sc)
ISBN: 979-8-8230-3078-6 (hc)
ISBN: 979-8-8230-3076-2 (e)

Library of Congress Control Number: 2024915226

Print information available on the last page.

This book is printed on acid-free paper.

Typist: Abigail Hughes

Dedication

I dedicate this book to my beloved husband, Frank, with all of my love. He always encouraged me to write and wanted me to have a book of my poetry one day. Although he is no longer with us, I know one day God will reunite us.

IN LOVING MEMORY OF FRANK KEATON

My dad left for his heavenly home on February 6, 2022. My family and I want to thank everyone who prayed for him and my mother. They were married almost 24 years. He was my stepdad and he showed me more love than words can say. His example of a Christian life will forever remain with me as his words, "never forget how much I love you, Marily" and "you are my baby girl"! I thank God for all the great times we had together, and I know I will see you again one day!

Love,
Marilyn 'Marily' Boughton

I also dedicate this book to my loving daughter, Marilyn, who I dearly love, and she has blessed my life. She is responsible for promising to make this book become a reality as a legacy for our family, including my grandchildren and great-grandchildren.

And I also dedicate this book to my son-in-law, Joe, who has helped me in so many ways and treats me like his own mother.

My sincere thanks I give to God, who has inspired me, saved me, and given me a wonderful long life. I give thanks to Him for each day of life and for my family and friends. He blessed me with the gift of poetry, for which I am forever grateful. I pray these God given words might bring someone to know God.

Acknowledgements

This book would never have happened if not for my daughter, Marilyn, and my son-in-law, Joe, who believed in me and wanted this for me for many years.

To my parents, Bertha and Charlie, whose love and Christian upbringing helped form me into the person God created me to be.

I want to thank one of my best friends, Ivy Day, a gospel singer from Ohio, who has recorded numerous songs and several from my poems.

A special thanks to Teresa Cartwright Baldwin, author of "I am Clay", who shared information and lead me to AuthorHouse.

And to Abigail Hughes, the sweetest and kindest young lady who typed all of my poetry from my handwritten notes and somehow managed to read my writing. I was so blessed to have her help.

A Dream From God

On my knees by my bed,
You should have heard what Jesus said.
As I prayed 'bout a dream I'd had,
He said, "if you'll stay true to me,
God's great kingdom you will see.
And in your robe of white you'll be clad."

"Do all you can while you're on Earth,
To win your family to new birth.
As you walk hand in hand with me,
Pray to God day and night,
As you walk in His light,
And Heaven's treasures will be guaranteed."

This dream was so real,
Jesus' presence I could feel.
Praise the Lord, He saved my soul.
He took away all strife,
And He gave me a brand new life.
Glory to God I've been made whole.

Chorus:

My Father's riches of pure gold,
The greatest story ever told.
How He died upon that tree,
Just to save you and me.
No more sickness we'll bare,
We'll all be shouting over there.
What a glorious day that will be.

J Remember The Night Jesus Saved Me

I remember the night Jesus saved me,
I was visiting at my brother's home.
I wanted to talk to my brother,
But ole Satan wouldn't leave us alone.

We rebuked him in the name of Jesus.
I began to pray aloud.
The fire fell from heaven all around me,
I felt that I was floating on a cloud.

I made a promise to God the Father.
"To Him I will always be true"
I'll live for Him the rest of my life,
And I'll do what He wants me to do.

Chorus:

Yes, I remember the night Jesus saved me
Now my name is in the Lambs' Book of Life
I heard a sweet voice saying, "make me your choice"
And I entered His arms within.

My Personal Testimony

When I was lost, God spoke to me.
Then I knelt down on bended knee.
I prayed, "oh Lord, please forgive me,
And I will always live for Thee."

I'm happy now I trusted him.
Before I prayed my way was dim.
My life is brighter every day
Because He washed my sins away.

I could not have the things I do
If I hadn't put my trust in you.
I thank you Lord for saving me.
Praise God, I know that I am free.

Chorus:

Yes, Jesus cared and He saved me.
Just ask of Him and you will see,
How happy life will always be.
Thank God, I know that you saved me.

On My Way to Heaven

I'm on my way to Heaven,
I'm just passing through.
I want to see my Jesus,
How about you?

He's waiting to see us,
Through the Pearly Gates.
See our saved loved ones,
Won't that be great?

Oh, praise the name of Jesus,
He's worthy of our praise.
Let's thank Him for His goodness,
All of our days.

He said He's coming back,
To take His children Home.
We'll live there forever,
In our Heavenly Home.

God's Creations

The warm sunshine in spring,
Bring the birdies out to sing,
Pretty flowers everywhere,
Smells so sweet in summer air.

Soft clouds in the skies,
Mornin's beautiful sunrise,
The rivers and the streams,
Are a fishermans dreams.

Wild berries in the field,
A good crop you can yield.
In the orchard apples mellow,
Red delicious and golden yellow.

In the garden ripe tomatoes,
In a ridge are sweet potatoes.
Bunch beans for winter feed,
Save a few for next years seed.

All God's works we plainly see,
From Mankind to the tallest tree.
Our Thanks go to God alone,
A wonderful world and a precious home.

I'm Ready to Leave This World

Jesus died for me when He hung upon that tree
Oh the pain He suffered for me
I got down on my knees, I said, "Jesus, will you please?"
Forgive me and He saved me.

I was happy that day when He washed my sins away
I'm going to Heaven some day
I'll see the Father and His Son after this old race is won
I'm ready to leave this world.

The things here on Earth don't compare to my new birth
I'm longing to see Jesus' face
My mother and my dad, brother, sister that I had
Are waiting in Heaven for me.

Chorus:

I'm ready to go, my Jesus told me so
I'm ready to leave this world
Leaving sorry and pain, I have so much to gain
I'm ready to leave this world.

Heavenly Home

I'm traveling the straight and narrow way
I'll walk with you Lord, all the way.
Heaven is my home I'm waiting to see.
Thank you Lord for saving me.

A beautiful life we'll have up there
Nothing on Earth could ever compare.
Jesus will call me, it won't be long.
He will take us to our Heavenly Home.

Heaven

I'm thinking of Heaven tonight
While the stars are shining so bright
Is Heaven really that far away?
I wonder 'cause I'm going someday.

Jesus took all my burdens away
When He saved me that wonderful day
Waiting and watching the Eastern sky
I'll leave here in the twinkling of an eye.

It is well with my soul, I know
When He saved me, He told me so
Mom and Dad are waiting for us all
We will go when Jesus makes the call.

I'm Living For Jesus Now

I used to sin, 'till Jesus came in,
In Him, I found sweet peace.
I've joy in my soul,
Since Jesus made me whole,
I'm living for Jesus now.

We'll hear the Angels band, in Heaven's fair land,
If we keep pressing on,
When this life here is done,
The battle we have won,
If we're living for Jesus now.

No one could be so precious to me,
The Comforter has come,
On that Golden Shore,
Where we'll weep no more,
If we're living for Jesus now.

I'm gonna shout and sing until the Heavens ring,
To glorify His name,
Since Jesus saved me,
I'm happy as can be,
I'm living for Jesus now.

Chorus:

I'm on the winning side,
In Jesus I abide,
Praise His Holy Name,
When I hear that trumpet sound,
I'll be Heaven bound,
I'm living for Jesus now.

A Closer Walk

When I'm down in the valley, my Jesus I can see,
I look up toward Heaven, and He's smiling down at me.
When I'm discouraged and don't know what to do,
I call out to Jesus, I need a closer walk with You.

I can't wait to see my home up in Heaven so fair,
And see precious Jesus descending in air.
I know my Mother's waiting on that Golden Avenue.
Oh Lord, I have to have a little closer walk with You.

I feel close to You Jesus, in our walk everyday,
I'm not perfect, I know, but in Your will I want to stay.
When I stumble and fall I can depend on You,
Oh Lord I just want a little closer walk with You.

Chorus:

Just a closer walk with you, Lord,
Is what I want today,
I didn't start this walk for nothing.
Im going all the way.
I'll keep my eyes on You, Lord,
And I'll never be untrue,
'Cause all that I want is a closer walk with You.

11

Praise Jesus

In the Lamb's Book of Life,
My name is written there,
I surrendered all to Jesus,
And I left my burdens there.

Oh His name I'll praise forever,
He has done so much for me,
In His footsteps I will follow,
As I pray down on my knees.

Thank You Jesus

I thank you Jesus for dying for me.
You shed your blood, so I could go free.
From the sins of the world and life I live,
So much I ask, and so little I give.

I pray that you will believe in me,
That I want to be saved and live for thee.
Just cleanse my heart 'til it's white as snow,
Then I'll know I'm ready to go.

13

Oh How Sweet The Walk With Jesus

Oh how sweet the walk with Jesus,
It gets sweeter everyday.
When He puts His arms around me,
I know things will be okay.

I always want to serve You, Lord.
As I travel life's highway.
How sweet the walk with Jesus,
It gets sweeter everyday.

Oh I want to see You, Jesus
And look upon Your face
I think of what You've done for me
With Your amazing grace

I will praise You, Lord, forever.
You have been so good to me.
Oh how sweet the walk with Jesus.
And to know that I'm set free.

Chorus:

Oh how sweet the walk with Jesus
And to know my sins are gone
He cast them in the deep, deep sea
I'm making Heaven my home
Now my name is in the Book of Life
And Jesus holds the key
Oh how sweet the walk with Jesus
And to know that He loves me

Praise His Name

I was brought up in a Christian home
I was taught right from wrong
Now I am saved by His grace — Praise His name
He filled my heart with love and joy
I never get tired of the old, old story
I'm living for Jesus everyday. Praise His name.

He has been so good to me
Healing my eyes so I can see
When I am down I call on Him — Praise His name
There's nothing like my time with Him
Because He saved me from my sin
All my life I owe to Him. Praise His name.

Chorus:

Oh glory to His name let the Hallelujahs ring
The brand new song we will sing
Not even the angels know this song
It was written for God's children alone
Will praise His name up on high
We'll be in Heaven by and by.

The Lord Has Been So Good To Me

The Lord has been so good to me. I cannot tell it all.
When sickness and discouragement comes
and my backs against the wall.
I go down on my knees to God in prayer
he knows sometimes I fall,
The Lord has been so good to me I cannot tell it all.

The enemy came to me and said "you know you'll never last"
I said, "Satan, you're a liar. God forgave me of my past."
He came again and said to me, "I'll show you a better way"
I said, " I love Jesus and I'm going all the way."

I trust in the Lord with all my Heart. He hears my every prayer
He's brought me through some trying
times. I know He's always there.
He's the First and Last, the Great I Am,
there's much more I recall
The Lord has been so good to me, I cannot tell it all.

Going Home With Jesus

I'm going home with Jesus, I want to see the King.
I'm going home with Jesus, to hear the Angels sing.
When Gabriel blows His trumpet, I'll go sailing through the sky.
I'm going home with Jesus, bidding this old world goodbye.

He washed away my sins, they're white as snow.
He saved and sanctified me a long time ago.
I daily walk beside Him as onward I go.
I'm going home with Jesus, the Bible tells me so.

I'll sing with the Angels God's new song.
Written for God's people as we gather around the throne.
When I see my loved ones, what a joyous time.
Then Jesus calls His children, come and dine.

We'll sit at the Master's table with Matthew, Luke, and John.
Maybe sit by Jesus as time goes on.
He will show me to my mansion He's prepared for me.
I'm going home with Jesus, I've been set free.

Jesus Means Everything To Me

I cannot wait to see Jesus
And look upon His face
When this old life is over
We'll go to a better place
Our treasures up in Heaven
Are waiting there you see
I can't begin to tell you
He means everything to me.

He sanctified me wholly
Now I'm a child of the King
I was baptized in His Spirit
Can't you hear the angels sing?
Another child is coming home
Write my name for all to see
I tell you my Jesus
He means everything to me.

Chorus:

Jesus is my rock
I lean on everyday
He's there when I am praying
To take my cares away
I'll walk close beside Him
The enemy must flee
I tell you my Jesus
Means everything to me.

18

Praise The Name Of Jesus

I was in the world of sin
When Jesus spoke to me
He said get your life in order
If you want to see me.

I thought that I had lots of time
But he revealed to me
Todays the day of Salvation,
And you can go free.

So I got down on my knees
And gave my heart to God.
Jesus said if you daily walk with me,
On streets of gold you'll trod.

He said I've built you a home in Heaven.
I shed my blood at Calvary
I said thank you, praise you Jesus.
You mean everything to me.

Chorus:

I will praise the name of Jesus
Till he takes me home.
Oh Lord I'm getting anxious
To see my Heavenly Home.

You Better Get On Fire For God

I want to be in that number,
When the Saints go marching in.
I want to see my Jesus.
He died for my sins.
I want to see those streets of gold,
On them I will trod.
If you want to go to Heaven,
You better get on fire for God.

Ole Satan tries to rule this world,
He thinks he is boss.
Jesus has more power,
He showed him on the cross.
Let us tell all the world,
Both here and abroad,
If you want to go to Heaven,
You better get on fire for God.

When Jesus splits the eastern sky,
I'm leaving this old Earth,
To be with Him forever.
He gave me new birth.
The pearly gates will open wide,
Over Heaven I'll trod.
I'm gonna make it to Heaven,
I'm on fire for God.

Chorus:

If you want to know Jesus,
You better kneel down and pray.
Ask Him into your heart,
Then just obey.
The angels in Heaven,
Will rejoice and applaud.
If you want to go to Heaven,
You better get on fire for God.

What Would You Give In Exchange For Your Soul

What would you give in exchange for your soul
Do you want to see Jesus? His book to enroll.
Just plead the blood of Jesus and leave Him in control.
What would you give in exchange for your soul?

What would you give in exchange for your soul
A sinful life will soon take its toll.
Just cry out to Jesus, to Him pray through
He died on the cross for me and for you.

There's nothing more precious than God's saving grace
Someday we will meet him face to face.
Friend, take a firm stand while seeing your goal
What would you give in exchange for your soul?

Listen closely, do you hear a small voice?
Saying come to me, make me your choice.
If you follow Jesus, you'll have self control
What would you give in exchange for your soul?

Chorus:

Has the things of this world got you out of control?
Think, where would you be if you lost your soul?
Come to Jesus today, He will make you whole.
What would you give, if you lost your soul?

Plead The Blood Of Jesus

Invitation Song

Jesus is waiting for His children to come home,
Children, are you ready, don't be left alone.
The days are surely on us from the Bible we've read,
Get on your knees and repent, that's what Jesus said.

I read about Brother Job, the trials he went through,
He lost his fame and fortune, but to God he stayed true.
When life doesn't seem fair, don't give up the fight.
God is there for you, to save you tonight.

Chorus:

Just plead the blood of Jesus and receive Him tonight.
He wants to save you, He'll make things alright.
Just plead the blood of Jesus and seek His face.
He loves you, He will save you by His grace.

Take It To Jesus In Prayer

Take it to Jesus, take it to Jesus
Take it to Jesus in prayer.
When you are troubled
Still you must care.
Just take it to Jesus in prayer.

When troubles of this world
Are more than you can bare
Take it to Jesus in prayer.
Stand on His word
Our burdens he will bare
If you'll take it to Jesus in prayer

When our sins are all forgiven
And He comes in the air
We'll leave this old world
A white robe we'll wear
Let us praise Him, he really cares.
Take it to Jesus in prayer

Chorus:

Take it to Jesus
Take it to Jesus
Take it to Jesus in prayer
Get down on your knees
He will meet you there
If you'll take it to Jesus in prayer

I'm Leaving It All In Jesus' Hands

What a Savior, what a friend,
With His love there is no end,
There's no other who cares so much for me.
All my burdens He does bare,
'Cause I took 'em to Him in prayer,
I'm leaving it all in Jesus' hands.

When my way seems dark as night,
He will lead me in His light,
From the valley to the mountain so high.
On no other I depend,
I'll stick with Jesus till the end,
I'm leaving it all in Jesus' hands.

When the rapture takes place,
I know I'll see my Savior's face,
I will meet up with Jesus in the air.
As we walk along that shore,
I'll be with Him forevermore,
I'm leaving it all in Jesus' hands.

Chorus:

I'm leaving it all in Jesus' hands,
I'll obey all His commands,
He said I can go to the Glory Land,
If I leave it all in Jesus' hands.

Lord I Cannot Wait

Oh my Lord I cannot wait,
Until the day you take me home.
Can't wait to see your precious face,
And to know this Earth I'll no more roam.

I know my Mother's waiting there,
She's pleading children follow me.
I want us to be in Heaven,
Gathering round that Crystal Sea.

When the Pearly Gates swing open wide,
I'm gonna be on the winning side.
And hear my Jesus say well done,
The race on Earth you now have won.

Chorus:
I'm going Home to be with Jesus,
To see the mansions in the sky,
With Jasper walls and streets of gold,
Most Precious Story ever told.

Jesus I Love You

Oh Jesus I love, love, love you
I can't get enough, enough of you
I want to know more, more about you
You are amazing to me.

How you made this world, it's a mystery to me.
How you made the mountains and the sea
The sun and moon to give us light
The sun in the day and moon at night.

How you hung the stars in the sky
Twinkling at night so very high
Beautiful flowers, streams and trees
All for your children to see.

Someday I'll be there and it won't be long
I'm passing my time writing this song
My house is in order I've made it so
My sins are gone, they're white as snow.

Chorus:

I'm ready and waiting for the day
When I can hear my Jesus say
I'm taking you home with me on high
Where you never, never will die.

Homecoming Day

Jesus is calling His children home,
Our loved ones are there, we won't be alone.
If you're saved, you're on your way,
To that wonderful Homecoming Day.

Peace

Start your day the blessed way
With Jesus on your mind.
Pray each day that troubles go away,
Then peace on earth you'll find.

My Destination

My destination is Heaven,
His Kingdom I desire.
The enemy won't get me,
To put in his fire.

I've made myself ready,
A long time ago.
Jesus sure loves me,
The Bible tells me so.

What Would I Do

What would I do, oh what would I do?
What would I do, without Jesus?
He's my shining light both day and night.
What would I do, without Jesus?

I need Him by my side, both night and day,
There's so much more that I could say.
He opens blind eyes and makes the mute to talk,
I'll stay in His Word, with Him I will walk.

Repeat:

What would I do, oh what would I do?
What would I do, without Jesus?
He's my shining light both day and night.
What would I do, without Jesus?

Win A Soul

Love your neighbor as yourself, help them make it in,
Time is short, let's get to work, and get them saved from sin.
Lord, lay someone on my heart so I can lead them to you,
I'd rather be a Soul Winner than anything else I do.

Heaven On My Mind

I'm thinking tonight about Heaven.
I have family up there I know.
I cannot wait to see them,
Seems they have been gone so long.

When we gather around God's throne,
In our robes of white we will wear.
We'll meet all the Saints of Old,
And no one will have a care.

I'm Going Home

I'm going home with Jesus
When my time is up.
We'll gather around His table
With Him we will sup.

What a meeting that will be,
To see all our loved ones there.
All the old saints of the Bible,
They will all be there.

What a wonderful time we will have
Walking the streets of gold.
Pearly Gates and Jasper Walls,
The half has never been told.

Lord Teach Me

Oh Lord, teach me how to be more like you.
Teach me to love everyone like you do.
Lord teach me how to have patience like Job.
Teach me to give you my heavy load.

Just mold me the way you want me to be.
Teach me to pray with sincerity.
Teach me to walk with you hand in hand.
I will obey your every command.

Chorus:

Teach me Oh Lord
I'll listen to you
I'll do anything
You want me to do
I'll go the extra mile
Any day for you
Just teach me Oh Lord
To be more like you.

The Day He Died On Calvary

Let me tell you a story,
About one who died for me,
To save me from sin,
So I could be free,
He paid my debt,
When He hung on that tree,
The day He died on Calvary.

A crown of thorns around His head,
Pierced His skin until it bled,
They cursed Him and mocked Him,
On Calvary,
He cried Father forgive them,
For they know not what they do,
Then He died for me and you.

They laid Him in the tomb,
Rolled the stone to the door,
They thought they would never,
See Jesus any more.
When two women went to the grave,
The stone was rolled away,
Jesus had risen and He's alive today.

He's alive He's alive,
Interceding for me,
At the right hand of my Father,
Like He said He'd be,
How can we turn Him away,
After all He went through,
He wants to save us, and,
I'm glad I've prayed through.

Chorus:

He was falsely accused,
And hated by the Jews,
No mercy did they show for Him,
A heavy whip they did crack,
Cut bloody stripes upon His back,
Then He died on Calvary.

Pray

Don't worry about tomorrow
We wasn't guaranteed today.
Just put your faith in Jesus
And pray, pray, pray.

Put your faith in Jesus
He's the only way
We'll go home with Him,
Some sweet day.

Watch the eastern sky,
He could be coming soon.
If we're ready, we'll go with Him,
Sailing thru the blue.

Thank You Lord

I thank you Lord for dying for me.
You shed your blood so I could go free.
From the sins of the world and life I live.
So much I ask and so little I give.

I pray that you will believe in me.
That I want to be saved and live for thee.
Just cleanse my heart till its white as snow.
Then I'll know that I'm ready to go.

Thinking Of Heaven

Lord, I'm thinking of Heaven today.
I know time is not so far away.
I want to be ready when you come,
All our work on Earth will be done.

So we'll work, we'll work 'till Jesus comes.
Singing praises to the Father and the Son,
Draw me nearer, nearer everyday.
So I'll be prepared to meet you on that day.

Holy Spirit, Holy Spirit guide my way,
Go before me each and everyday,
Keep me on the straight and narrow way.
And I'll go with You, with You all the way.

Matthew Twenty-Four

I believe the good old Bible from beginning to the end.
I believe the Lord is coming back for you and me, my friend.
I believe that he is knocking on everyone's door.
You can read it all in Matthew twenty-four.

There'll be wars and rumors of wars and
earthquakes in diver's places.
Love will grow cold among all the races.
False prophets will appear, don't believe, just ignore.
It tells all about it in Matthew twenty-four.

There'll be trials and tribulations, time is drawing mighty near.
These things will come to pass, his word we must fear.
Put your faith and trust in Jesus, His spirit He'll outpour.
Read all about it in Matthew twenty-four.

The Holy book is precious, God's promises are true.
What He's done for others, He'll surely do for you.
He'll open up the Heavens, pour out blessings galore.
Pick up your Bible and read Matthew twenty-four.

Friend, get your life in order, Jesus is coming very soon.
It might be night or it might be noon,
But there's one thing for certain, you can live forever more.
Get out your Bible, read Matthew twenty-four.

Chorus:

Pick up your Bible and read the Holy word.
His treasures in Heaven He said would be assured.
If you'd ask for forgiveness when he knocks at your door,
It's all written there in Matthew twenty-four.

Jesus I Love You

Oh Jesus I love, love, love you
I can't get enough, enough of you
I want to know more, more about you
You are amazing to me.

How you made this world, it's a mystery to me.
How you made the mountains and the sea
The sun and moon to give us light
The sun in the day and moon at night.

How you hung the stars in the sky
Twinkling at night so very high
Beautiful flowers, streams and trees
All for your children to see.

Someday I'll be there and it won't be long
I'm passing my time writing this song
My house is in order I've made it so
My sins are gone, they're white as snow.

My Family In Heaven Is Waiting For Me

My family in Heaven is waiting for me.
I'll be there to meet them some day.
Would you wait for me by the Crystal Sea?
I'll be there to meet you some day.

I know it wont be long, let's all stay strong.
We'll make it to Heaven some day.
This world is not my home, I'll no longer roam,
I'm going to Heaven some day.

Jesus Is Coming

Jesus is coming,
He's coming very soon.
It might be night,
Or it might be noon.
You can be sure
His promises are true.
Hes coming again
For me and for you.

Yes, Jesus is coming
To take us home.
For all His children
This Earth no more roam.
He's coming to receive us
Like a thief in the night.
Jesus is coming
And it might be tonight.

So get your life in order,
Get your family saved.
The Bible is our road map,
The road's already paved.
Read 1st John I nine,
He'll forgive your sin.
Then live your life for Jesus,
The battle you will win.

Wanna See My Family

Gates of Pearl, streets of Gold
Jasper walls I've been told
A new mansion built for me
Beautiful flowers for me to see

I'm going there some sweet day
To be with Jesus every day
Wanna see my family that I had
Ray, Winona, Mom, and Dad

Frank is waiting there for me
He said he'd wait by the Crystal Sea
I cannot wait to see him again
We'll be together until the end.

I'm Living For Jesus Now

I used to sin, 'till Jesus came in,
In Him, I found sweet peace.
I've joy in my soul,
Since Jesus made me whole,
I'm living for Jesus now.

We'll hear the Angels band, in Heaven's fair land,
If we keep pressing on,
When this life here is done,
The battle we have won,
If we're living for Jesus now.

No one could be so precious to me,
The Comforter has come,
On that Golden Shore,
Where we'll weep no more,
If we're living for Jesus now.

I'm gonna shout and sing until the Heavens ring,
To glorify His name,
Since Jesus saved me,
I'm happy as can be,
I'm living for Jesus now.

Chorus:

I'm on the winning side,
In Jesus I abide,
Praise His Holy Name,
When I hear that trumpet sound,
I'll be Heaven bound,
I'm living for Jesus now.

Praise His Name

I was brought up in a Christian home
I was taught right from wrong
Now I am saved by His grace — Praise His name
He filled my heart with love and joy
I never get tired of the old, old story
I'm living for Jesus everyday. Praise His name.

He has been so good to me
Healing my eyes so I can see
When I am down I call on Him — Praise His name
There's nothing like my time with Him
Because He saved me from my sin
All my life I owe to Him. Praise His name.

Chorus:

Oh glory to His name let the Hallelujahs ring
The brand new song we will sing
Not even the angels know this song
It was written for God's children alone
I will praise His name up on high
We'll be in Heaven by and by.

Heaven

I'm thinking of Heaven tonight
While the stars are shining so bright
Is Heaven really that far away?
I wonder 'cause I'm going someday.

Jesus took all my burdens away
When He saved me that wonderful day
Waiting and watching the Eastern sky
I'll leave here in the twinkling of an eye.

It is well with my soul, I know
When He saved me, He told me so
Mom and Dad are waiting for us all
We will go when Jesus makes the call.

Jesus You're My Savior

Lord You loved me as a sinner,
You saw something good in me,
You reached down from Heaven,
And graciously Saved me.
I owe my life to You Lord,
That's the way it's gonna be,
Jesus You're my Savior,
I know You set me free.

I cannot live without you, Lord,
I want You living in my heart,
I'll always walk beside You,
Never to be apart,
Lord, I cannot wait to see You.
And look upon Your shining face,
And reign with You forever,
In that beautiful Heavenly place.

Glory Hallelujah,
I just want to praise Your name,
You're the rock that I lean on,
You're my sunshine in the rain.
You mean everything to me Lord,
I love you more everyday,
I won't live without You,
I'm going home with You someday.

Chorus:

Jesus You're my Savior,
You're my Lord of everything,
I'll praise Your name forever,
You are the reigning King.
Yes I know that You love me,
You picked me up when I was low,
You cleansed me with Your blood,
And washed me whiter than the snow.

Jesus You're Lord Of My Life

Chorus:

Jesus You're Lord of my life,
Jesus You're Lord of my life,
When I heard you call,
I made you Master of all,
Jesus You're Lord of my life.

I remember the night Jesus saved me,
I was sad, heavy, laden with sin,
When I heard a sweet voice,
Saying make me your choice,
I let Jesus dwell here within.

There are days we all can remember,
But there are some we'd like to forget,
Jesus remembers our sins no more,
On Calvary, He paid our debt.

Now I'm walking each day hand in hand,
With my Savior, I know He's in command,
Praise His Holy name,
I will never be the same,
Jesus You're Lord of my life.

Keep Your Eyes On Jesus

Keep your eyes on Jesus,
He will always see you through.
Get on your knees and ask Him,
And start your life anew.

On the cruel cross of Calvary,
Jesus died for you and me.
On His back the stripes for healing,
He is waiting to heal you.

Sin is pleasure for a season,
Don't partake of the world.
The enemy is lurking,
To keep your life a whirl.

Can You Imagine What Heaven Is Like?

Can you imagine what Heaven is like?
Can you imagine a day without night?
Swing the gates open wide,
Leave the enemy outside.
Can you imagine what Heaven is like?

Paint a picture of Jesus on the throne,
And hear Him say, "my children, welcome home."
I have your mansion on a hill,
So peaceful and still.
Can you imagine what Heaven is like?

I'm going home to be with Jesus, I know.
How do I know, the Bible tells me so.
He forgave me of my sins,
When I invited Him in.
Can you imagine what Heaven is like?

Chorus:
How beautiful Heaven must be,
Too beautiful for man's eyes to see,
But we'll be changed in the twinkling of an eye,
When we meet our Jesus in the sky.

Jesus Is My Rock

Jesus is my rock, my name is on the roll.
I'm so glad He saved me a long, long time ago.
He said if I would follow Him, His Kingdom I would see.
I know He died upon that cross to set His people free.

Jesus is my rock, my name is on the roll.
It's written in the Book of Life that satisfies my soul.
If I can stand the storms of life as onward I go,
My reward will be in Heaven, 'cause my name is on the roll.

Jesus is the winner, Satan He did defeat.
The only place for Satan is under my feet.
I will defeat the enemy as onward I go.
Thank God I know my name is written on the roll.

I'll praise His name forever, He has been so good to me.
I know He's always with me when I am on my knees.
This world we live in has taken its toll.
Thank God for my Savior, my name is on the roll.

Jesus' Precious Blood

The precious blood of Jesus has saved my wretched soul.
His blood has healed my body and made my body whole.
I'll praise the name of Jesus until my dying day.
I will daily walk beside Him; I'm going all the way.

I'm going to that city for eternal life with Him,
It is promised in His word if we're saved from our sin.
We can Know we are saved, 'cause His Spirit lives within,
Let our light shine so others make it in.

Walking With Jesus

I am praying to you, Jesus, at my bedside every night.
For I need you more than ever, like the blind man needed sight.
I had thought about repenting, but had lived in sin so long,
To ask You for forgiveness, now I know it wasn't wrong.

Then a sweet noise spoke so softly and
with tender words did say,
I'll forgive you of your past if you will listen and obey.
I accepted what He offered and I got my reward,
That's why I'm walking in the light, I'm living for my Lord.

I am walking in the light that my Savior shined for me.
I am walking in His footsteps for His Glory Land to see.
Yes, I'm walking in His shadow, for it is the only way.
I thank God that I can do so, 'cause He washed my sins away.

Yes, I'm saved, I'm born again, I'm living better everyday.
What a difference in my life, since my sins were washed away.
A new home prepared for me with streets paved with gold.
This is my personal testimony, my story I have told.

Going Home

I've got a friend in Jesus, He's been so good to me.
When I need Him most, He meets me on my knees.
I'll never forsake Him, I need Him everyday.
I cannot live without Him, His word I'll obey.

One of these days, I'm going home with Him,
Because He saved me from all of my sin.
I'll praise his name forever, He means everything to me.
He's waiting to take me home to see my family.

The Angels in Heaven are waiting for me,
Dressed in beautiful garments for me to see.
My name is on my mansion above the door,
I'll live there forever and forever more.

Praise the name of Jesus, I'm ready to go home.
This old Earth I've traveled but I'll never more roam.
He said in His word He's coming back again,
Since I'm free of my sins, I'm going home with Him.

That Great Judgement Day

On that Great Judgement Day,
I want to hear Jesus say,
"Brother and Sister come on in,
I forgave you of your sins."
Well done child of God,
On this Earth no more you'll trod.
Let's get ready for
That Great Judgement Day.

No more sickness, no more dying.
No more tears, no more crying.
In that land of milk and honey,
We won't need any money.
Now if your name is written there,
You will never have a care.
You better get ready for
That Great Judgement Day.

Church get ready for that day,
Let Him wash your sins away.
You will praise His Holy name,
And you'll never be the same.
He will have you a place on high,
You can bid this world goodbye.
You better get ready for
That Great Judgement Day.

He's coming soon, this I know,
And I am ready to go.
The Holy Spirit revealed to me,
That my faith has set me free.
The signs of time are everywhere,
A robe of white for us to wear.
You better get ready for
That Great Judgement Day.

Chorus:

The Holy Spirit is everywhere,
He will hear your faintest prayer.
God gave His son to die for me,
And by faith He set me free.
Trust in Him, He'll take you through,
But to Him you must be true.
You better get ready for
That Great Judgement Day.

My Jesus

Since my Jesus saved me,
I've never been the same.
I raise my hands toward Heaven,
I praise His Holy name.
Oh, Satan tried to tell me,
That I am not God's own.
I said, "you are a liar,
You better leave God's children alone."

When I need my Jesus,
I go down on my knees.
I know that He hears me,
He's the one that set me free.
I put my trust in Jesus,
A long, long time ago.
My prayers go to Heaven,
This I surely know.

My name is up in Heaven,
Soon I'll be going there.
Jesus is coming for me,
I'll meet Him in the air.
Quickly I'll be taken,
Because I'm free from all sin.
Forever to be with Jesus,
Heaven's gates I'll enter in.

Chorus:

He's still on the throne,
Interceding for me.
At the right hand of the Father,
Who loves you and me.
Come and go with me,
Be a child of the King.
My home is up in Heaven,
Where I'll hear the angels sing.

Jesus Helped Me

I'd like to take some time to rest my mind.
Forget it all, put it all behind.
Sometimes, I thought I couldn't go on,
Jesus said, "I'll help you, keep going on."

The trouble and heartache I've been through,
Jesus said, "I'll fix it, I'll make it all new."
He said, "Put it behind you, do the best you can."
"I'll be there with you holding your hand."

He's such a big part of my life.
He can take away trouble, heartache, and strife.
I answered His call when He knocked at my door.
I'll love Him forever and forever more.

King James Bible

Pastor Keith, you taught me well.

King James Bible is our road map to home
Read it and study it, you can't go wrong
I want the words just right when I read
It's just exactly what I need.

That's the good Bible we all can enjoy
Read it everyday, there's lots of good stories
God's right there to save from sin
Let your light shine so others make it in

When my Jesus saved me, He made me whole
Reading King James satisfies my soul
I made myself ready a long time ago
When the death angel comes, I'm ready to go.

Amen

Worry And Fear

I don't need to worry and I don't need to fear,
So why do I do it when Jesus is near?
He can take it all away and dry my tears,
As time goes by, it could add me years.

When my time is up and I must go,
I'll leave Earthly things, this I know.
They don't mean a thing, I have treasures above,
I'll see my Jesus and my family I love.

Chorus:

So don't worry - and don't fear,
Jesus is willing, open your ear.
Thank Him and praise Him, He's always near.
You won't have to worry and won't have to fear.

Getting Anxious

Oh Lord I'm getting anxious
Is my work down here done?
Lord I'm looking for you
This race is almost run

Just build me a little cabin
In the corner of Glory Land
Lord I'm getting anxious
To hear your Angel's band.

Lord I'm getting anxious
To hear the trumpet sound
And enter gates of pearl
And walk on Holy ground

I'll see my precious family
And walk streets of gold
I'm going home to Heaven
My story has been told.

No Grass Gonna Grow Over Me

There ain't no grass gonna grow over me
There ain't no grass gonna grow over me
I'm going high up in the sky
Where my soul will never die.

I want to see Jesus, He's number one.
Mom and dad, our family he won.
All the old saints thats over there
All new robes for us to wear.

I'm going high up in the sky,
Bidding this old world goodbye.
I cannot wait till I get there,
No more pain or sickness there.

Almost Home

If you're saved by God's Grace,
You will see His shining face.
And this Earth, you'll never more roam.
Just trust Him everyday,
And His word we must obey,
I believe we are almost home.

Since I've had a new birth,
I get homesick on this Earth.
I've been promised a brand new home.
Large or small I don't care,
I just want to make it there.
I believe we are almost home.

Chorus:

Almost home, yes almost home,
All our cares and worries will be gone.
We can sit at Jesus' feet,
The table is spread for us to eat.
I believe we are almost home.

A Family Christmas

I tell you, the Holidays seem unreal,
We all get together and have a big meal.
Most favorite holiday is Christmas time,
The children all come and that makes nine.

Kelly and Zach have Aryssa and Beau.
The kids want to stay when its time to go.
Joey and Jackie bing their three to the fold,
Kennedy, Payton, and Willow, they are good as gold.

Marilyn and Joe have plenty to eat,
From desserts, cakes, and plenty of meat.
The island is full of goodies galore,
You can't find room to set anymore.

My Marilyn

My child – I have one, she's a beautiful girl.
Long blonde hair that's easy to curl.
A perfect lady, she's tall and thin.
Beautiful, blue eyes, a dimple in her chin.

Twenty years old this gal of mine,
She's honest and true, now that's a good sign.
She listens to reason, has respect for me,
We love each other, that's how it should be.

I think of her all through the day,
Wishing she wasn't so far away.
I'll see her again when I go to shop,
I never fail her house to stop.

Or a trip to the doctor, I'd rather not go.
It's an excuse for me, I'll see her I know.
Maybe someday she'll live close by,
We'll be so happy, we'll try not to cry.

Marilyn

Marilyn

April one, nineteen fifty-three,
A happier day could never be.
Our baby girl was born to me,
We were a family now, us three.

We were happy with our baby girl,
Picking a name, our minds in a whirl.
Thinking hard we both knew,
Our precious baby would be Marilyn Sue.

She grew into a lady so fast it seems,
Making her own way, following her dreams.
She did it all and did it right,
She worked till wee hours in the night.

College education got her through,
She had more work than she could do.
She did it though and did it well,
I am so proud when I can tell.

This is my daughter, so sweet and kind,
She helps everyone and doesn't mind.
She's a Child of God, no one can deny,
We're all going to Heaven in a twinkling of an eye.

Marily

Oh, Marily, tell me you're not 62,
That makes your Mama old.
You know, sweet one, you look 31,
But my age, I never told.

If you look in the dictionary under class,
Someone said your name was there.
You are a beautiful lady, inside and out,
There is no one to whom you compare.

Me and your Daddy, in younger years,
Looked pretty good for our age.
We made the most beautiful baby on Earth,
God blessed you with a youthful age.

You are beautiful in mine and God's eyes for a lifetime.
Happy Birthday Marily, I love you.
Mommy

Baby Dearest

You are a treasure most people never find.
So precious to me, so sweet and kind.
I knew April first nineteen fifty three,
I would love you forever, my Baby.

We're getting older, it don't seem right.
You're so far away, I miss you each night.
I miss you always, but it's hard at night.
Seems I miss you more when I tell you goodnight.

May God watch over you every day,
And take all the hurt and pains away.
A homecoming is on the horizon, my dear.
Where never no more will we shed a tear.

I love you deeply,
Mommy Dearest

My Angel Marilyn

Marilyn did something I never thought she would,
An awesome thing, didn't think she could.
She has a heart, must be out of gold.
She kept the story, but recently told.

"I'm buying you a car," she said one day.
I said, "don't do that, there's no way,
You need one on which to depend."
I said, "how many people will that offend?"

She said, "it is your car, 'cause I love you."
And don't you know, it's a Camry brand new,
2014.5 with extras galore,
I never had a car I liked any more.

I can't wait to see it, it's black you know,
I want to see Marily first, you know.
Shes' the prize, an Angel, don't you see?
Sent from Heaven just for me.

Black Beauty is the name I gave,
Many years Marily did save.
She gave it to me for Mother's Day,
What a wonderful gift to give away.

Things Marily Does

I've been through it all, through it all.
Days and nights of worry, worst I ever saw.
I'm trying hard, trying everyday.
I'll reach my goal, some sweet day.

I told this to Jesus, I want depression to leave.
Never to come back, to make me grieve.
No anxiety, no heartache, no trouble, no strife.
I want to live comfortable the rest of my life.

If it wasn't for Marily, what would I do?
I would sit here all day with nothing to do.
She takes me everywhere I need to go.
I thank her and praise her, I love her so.

Marily works hard, seems I'm just first on her mind.
She takes me to my appointments, we make them on time.
She checks on me and brings me good food.
She's tired, I know, but always in a good mood.

To Marilyn, My Beautiful Daughter

Thank you Marilyn,
I love you so much

You're an awesome, awesome daughter,
You mean the world to me.
There is no one I know of,
That would buy a car for me.

The load is lifted, I see the light.
A brand new car, just in sight,
I love the driver more than the car,
Couldn't wait to hug you, you drove so far.

Over the mountains and valleys wide,
The laws of the land you did abide,
Marilyn, I have many joyous tears,
I know it will last me many years.

You took your money you saved for years,
And bought me a car so I'd have no fears.
The Lord sees this all you know,
You'll be blessed, my child, from head to toe.

Your professionalism got you a good deal,
You have a heart of gold and it is real.
Thank you, Marily, thank you so much.
You're an Angel from Heaven with an Angel's touch.

To Marilyn

A child, just six, you couldn't understand,
What Mommy and Daddy was going through.
Although we didn't get along,
We both sure did love you.

The love we had for each other,
Just didn't seem to last.
So we both went our separate ways,
Our love was in the past.

All through the years I had to work,
So we could have clothes to wear.
I didn't know I was being betrayed.
I took our marriage very sincere.

While I was at work the cat did play,
I know for certain you see,
He was seeing other women,
That he loved more than he loved me.

Behind my back, lies were told.
To keep me and you apart,
Why? Ill never understand.
It really broke my heart.

Years fly by so rapidly,
But we grew closer all the time.
I'm glad we learned to forget,
And put those painful years behind.

Before I close, just one more thing,
Honey, my love for you runs deep.
Always remember what Mommy said,
Everynight before you go to sleep.

If there's a Heaven's Hall of Fame,
Marilyn, you surely have a place.
For all your love and kindness,
Can never be erased.

I love you with all my heart.
Your Mommy

My Little Girl

God gave me the most precious gift,
A little girl, so sweet and so kind.
I couldn't ask for anything better,
And to know she's really mine.

You'll always be a part of me,
No matter how far apart.
I may not be able to hug you at night,
But you're always in my heart.

A daughter is a precious gift,
Nothing else can compare.
I'd like to be with you more,
Sometimes life isn't fair.

The bond between you and me,
Can't be broken, no matter what.
It's been there, "How many years?"
Oh well, since you were a little tot.

God knows best, have a great life,
We'll be together again someday,
In Heaven with Grandma and Grandpa,
On that great Resurrection Day.

I love you,
Mommy

Marilyn

I'd like to call back the years,
If I could hold back the tears,
And relive my life again.
I was the Mommy and Daddy too,
For my baby, Marilyn Sue.
I'd give her a life anew.

I'd be at home where Mommy belongs.
I'd sing my baby a Christian song,
As I rock her to sleep at night.
I'd bring her up in church you see,
That's the way it was with me,
That's the way all children should be.

I didn't do the right thing,
So it caused a lot of pain.
I've dealt with it all my life.
A little girl needs Mom and Dad,
When she doesn't, her life is sad.
I wasn't the Mommy she should have had.

I'd like to make things right,
So I can sleep well at night.
It was a long, long time ago.
The pain just won't go away,
So please forgive me today,
So the hurt will go away.

Marily, Don't Cry For Me

When I die, don't cry for me.
I've made it home with my family.
I'll be waiting to see you
When you come sailing through the blue.

It could happen any day.
Let's keep prayers up day by day.
This old world's in an awful mess.
In Heaven, we'll have no stress!

I Dreamed I Saw My Mother

I got to look into Heaven in a dream one night.
The Saints surrounding Jesus, oh what a beautiful sight.
Sweet music was playing as we gathered around God's throne.
I just can't wait till Jesus takes me home.

We were strolling over Heaven, just Jesus and me,
Admiring the fragrant flowers growing by the Crystal Sea.
Then I saw some loved ones who had gone on before,
And oh, there stood my Mother, that's who I was looking for.

Then I hugged my Mother, not a tear did we shed.
There'll be no tears in Heaven, that's what Jesus said.
No sickness nor sorrow will be in this place.
When the battle is over, you then have won the race.

Then I awoke from my sleep, I couldn't realize,
That this was just a dream, I didn't fantasize.
Even though a dream, I want it to come true.
It happened to me and it can happen to you.

I was at my Mother's side when Jesus called her home.
I said, "I'll meet you in Heaven, you won't be there alone."
Soon I will follow and all our family.
She gave a little smile and went out in eternity.

Chorus:

Jesus, dear Jesus, I praise your holy name.
Ever since you SAVED me, I've never been the same.
I'm waiting and watching, looking toward the Eastern sky.
I'm going home with Jesus, bidding this old world goodbye.

83

Bertha Lea Greene, Marge's Mother

Mother

Not another chum of ours,
Could take our mother's place.
Who of them could cook and sew,
And be in every place?

Always when she's needed most,
Working with a song.
Thinking of us always first,
Whatever comes along.

Not another chum of ours,
Has smiles as kind as Mother's,
And not a chum in all the world,
Thinks so much of others.

Daddy

I'd like to call back the years,
If I could hold back the tears,
And relive my childhood again.
I remember I was very young,
Those good church songs us kids sung,
While my daddy played the organ by ear.

We loved to hear our Daddy read,
His love and guidance we did need,
So we listened when he took his time for us.
Bedtime stories and the Bible he read,
Be good children, live for God he said.
We all prayed then hurried off to bed.

Chorus:

Oh what joy filled our heart,
With a good life we did start,
Precious Memories, say it all.
With five children and Mommy to feed,
Daddy worked hard, we were in need,
My Daddy set a good example for us all.

Charlie Jay Greene, Marge's Dad

My Dad

To My Daddy For Father's Day

My Dad is the most wonderful man,
That God ever created or ever can.
The things he does in his loving way,
Makes him special to me on this Father's Day.

Dad loved and cared for us children five.
With Mommy's help right by his side.
Before bedtime we'd all kneel to pray.
Then "hurry off to bed," we'd hear them say.

Daddy worked hard, brought things from the store,
With things going on like depression and war.
We survived very well I'm happy to say.
I love you so much Daddy, on this Father's Day.

My Daddy

My Daddy worked hard all his years.
Raising five children without any tears.
Oh there may have been some, he kept them hid.
They both worked hard to raise us kids.

We planted a big garden and canned a lot.
Then fed our pig with a bucket of slop.
When they got fat we'd butcher for meat.
You should have seen those hungry Greenes eat.

Mommy And Daddy

My Daddy would take me on his knee,
And read a Jesus story book to me.
He brought me up the way he should.
Mommy and Daddy always did the best they could.

We didn't have much, but we had love,
From Mommy and Daddy and Father above.
We prayed every night before going to sleep.
All five of us kids that Jesus would keep.

I remember well, Daddy reading each night,
Praying to make our light shine bright.
As I look back over years gone by,
I realize how hard my parents did try.

Us Three Kids

When I die, don't bury me
'Cause that ground is too cold for me.
I'm going high up in the sky
Where my soul will never die.

The Lord has been so good to me.
Also, my sister she's ninety-three.
In June my brother will be eighty-five.
I'm glad us three are still alive!

Mary and Bobby, Our Friends

We'll see you in Heaven, Bobby Hudson.

Now I have lost another friend
I'll keep holding on, it's not the end
Oh how it hurts to see them go
It leaves heartache, sorrow and woe

His wife has always been my best friend
And will always be until the end
Bobby and Mary were married seventy years
A lot they went through all those years.

Bobby was a Christian, that says a lot
A good example for all the little tots
We know he's well now, that was our wishes
He called Marilyn and Marge his Georgia peaches.

Ivy and Marge

Ivy and Marge are the best of friends.
When we get together conversation never ends.
We have so much to talk about,
Days aren't long enough, time runs out.

We've been friends for 30 years plus;
Never enough time for things to discuss.
When we get to Heaven we'll have time galore.
We'll be there forever and ever more.

Seems we went to Revivals most every night
Tim Case would preach, that guy's a sight.
We enjoyed the singing, preaching and all;
When Tim's around things never get dull.

But someday and not too long,
We'll all be singing God's new song.
One our ears have never heard,
All of it new, every word.

We'll see family and friends gone on before.
Looking around for our name over the door,
Of our Heavenly home, we can't wait to see
But Jesus is first for us to see.

We're looking for that day to come
When all our work down here is done.
We'll keep looking toward that Eastern sky,
Jesus will come in the twinkling of an eye.

Bernice

I pray this comforts Marilyn and Joe Boughton
God bless you for all you have done.
You are a wonderful daughter and I
love you and Joe very much.

Marilyn has always given of herself to others.
To everyone, friends and her mothers,
She dearly loved her mother in-law,
When she was in need, she gave her all.

She arranged for doctors, nurses, and all,
How many times did she make calls?
She set by her bedside read Bible verses,
She kept right on in spite of the nurses.

She arranged for Bernice to be brought home,
There is no place like home sweet home.
Marilyn fed her when she could eat,
And she stayed by her side with her hurting feet.

She had her cries, but knew it had to be done,
She stayed day and night till the race was won.
God called mom Home in the middle of the night.
That's the way she wanted it, it happened just right.

Marilyn, your reward in Heaven is great my dear,
Crying won't help so shed no more tears.
She's in Heaven now so her reward she did gain,
She has a new body with no more pain.

Bernice Boughton

A Mother so precious.
She had a heart of gold,
She will surely be missed,
By young and old.

But God had a plan,
We don't understand,
He needed an Angel,
In Heaven's Fair Land.

She was a strong woman,
Who really loved life,
Now she's in Heaven,
Where there's no more strife.

She has a new body,
No pain anymore,
She's sitting with Jesus,
Forever more.

When Jesus tugs at your heart,
Please let Him come in,
That's when He will SAVE you,
From all of your sin.

Doreen

Every two weeks Doreen comes to clean.
She cleans three floors, best you ever seen.
Her car got wrecked so I sold her mine.
She was desperate for one, and I didn't mind.

She starts out early and does all that.
She's got to make a living for her and her cat.
The cat will be waiting to welcome her in.
We treat our cats like family, is that a sin?

Margaret and Walt

Margaret and Walt were a beautiful pair.
Margaret was a beautician, she fixed hair.
She had her own shop that meant so much.
She was very good, she had the right touch.

She was the boss, she had girls galore.
Business was good, she didn't need anymore.
She even cooked for Walt, she was a good wife.
They loved each other all of their life.

Erla Spears

I love you Darlin'

Dearest Erla, my friend of 35 plus years,
You have made me very happy over the years.
You have cut my hair and highlighted it too,
I always liked a new hairdo.

We had lots of fun over the years.
You were a special lady with many peers.
You said Marge lets get a pedicure,
Something I had never endured.

"Let's go" you said and away we went
Over a half a day we had spent
You came out looking mighty fine.
Wasn't in there long, didn't take much time.

You suffered a lot but never complained
All of your pain you calmly contained
Kept working as long as you could;
You loved doing hair and you were good.

I'll never have an Erla hair cut again.
Erla was the best, always worked me in.
You were a friend I couldn't forget.
The nicest lady I ever met.

Forever Friends

Nancy and Marge, we're the best of friends.
When we're together, conversation never ends.
One of these days we're leaving this Earth.
We're going to Heaven, we have new birth.

Our names are written in the Lamb's Book of Life.
We'll be free of all heartache, trouble and strife.
We'll meet John and Frank on that Golden Shore,
And we'll be together forever more.

Our names on our mansion over the door
Written there for all of us four.
That's our new home up on the hill.
All the beauty of Heaven so quiet and still.

Linda Powell Was My Dearest Friend

My Sister in Christ Jesus

God must have needed an Angel,
So He called Sweet Linda Home.
No more pain no more suffering,
This Earth was not her home.

The short time that I knew her,
I loved her with all my heart.
An incredible woman much too young,
This world to depart.

But God knows all about it,
He has the last say.
Now she's in Heaven,
We'll see her again someday.

So if you're SAVED you'll see her too,
That's a promise God gave us all.
I've got lots of loved ones up there,
Someday, I'll get my call.

Minnie Merritt Went To Heaven

Minnie Merritt went to Heaven 10-15-2014
I love you Minnie.

Oh Minnie, what a good friend you have been
The incredible life you lived free of sin.
What a legacy you left for all to see
I know how you lived, you was a role model for me.

At songfest and revival's we enjoyed so much
Worshiping Jesus singing praises and such
Minnie, Ivy and Bertha you made my heart glad
Tim up there preaching with all the strength he had.

What a reunion we will have up there
No sickness no sorrow or pain to bare
Soon we will join you on that Golden Shore
Being with Jesus forever more.

The legacy you left your family, is richer than gold
No money could buy it, it's worth untold
How wonderful it will be, gold streets to roam
God must have needed an Angel, He called Minnie Home.

In Honor of J.D. Smith

J.D. we honor you today.
J.D. you're one of a kind.
When I think of a gentleman,
You come to my mind.

You are honest and good,
So polite to everyone.
We love you and Jane,
Our hearts you have won.

When Jesus is Lord of your life,
And our time on Earth is gone;
Heaven will be our reward
As Jesus will call us home.

God needed an Angel
He sent for you J.D.
We'll soon see you again
In Heaven by the Crystal Sea.

Our Pastor

Bro. Maggard you have taught and preached,
And won souls all around.
But we are selfish down here,
We still want you around.

We have loved you and respected you,
And admire all you have done.
Now your race is over.
Your Crown you have won.

But oh, how we miss you,
You was such a part of our life.
God must have needed an Angel,
And it took you dear life.

As I sit here just thinking,
You are in the presence of God.
No aches or pains,
On streets of gold you can trod.
You have loved ones up there
And souls that you won.
What a reunion for all,
The good work you have done.

For Brother and Sister Maggard

We appreciate you Pastor
We appreciate your wife.
Ever since I've been here,
You have strengthened my new life.

Pastor you're always looking
For some lost soul to save.
You're obedient to the Father
From His messages you gave.

You're always doing for others.
But leaving your wants behind.
You preach the Holy Word to us
No other Pastor is so kind.

Dr. Robert Sisk Saved My Eyes

I have Macular Degeneration in my right eye.
I now have 20/20 vision.

I had an eye problem in 2013
I needed a doctor so I could be seen
The first doctor said nothing can be done
I checked another place, I got someone

Cincinnati Eye Institute came to my mind
I got the best doctor anyone could find
Dr. Sisk said, "I can save your eye,
With three injections, want to try?"

I looked at Frank, we were in despair,
We hadn't heard of that, but I didn't care
I signed and three months my Retina was clear
Then later on something else did appear

The fluid and swelling won't go away
So I go every month to keep it at bay
I praise Dr. Sisk for saving my eye
If you need a Retina Doctor, give him a try

Tim

If you need something done, just call Tim,
He's a good worker, we all like him.
He reads his Bible everyday,
That's how you keep the devil away.

Abigail

We needed help typing, didn't know who to use.
Marilyn said, "I know, I'll call Abigail Hughes."
She's such a great worker, so good and kind.
The sweetest person you could ever find.

She came over after Marilyn gave her a call.
She knows her computer, she does it all.
The end of July, her school will start,
Then she has to leave, it will break my heart.

We're getting these poems ready for a book,
I didn't know so much it took.
Some are poems, some are a song,
We'll get them together where they belong.

Ruth Marie Moore

Ruth was Marge's cousin, whom she dearly loved.

Little Ruth Fawcett was two or three
Her mother gave her away so she could be free.
Of raising the child but she kept one
That broke Ruth's heart was nothing she'd done.

So sad a little girl was given away
She had a sister but she got to stay.
The little girl was given to an old couple to raise
Sweet as she could be in her childish ways.

Our family would go down, us kids would play
Always had fun on that special day.
She was born in Adams County and so was I
Didn't know then our bond would tie.

We grew older kinda lost track
But last few years our memories came back.
We talked on the phone some visits too
Even went to Frisch's for some good stew.

On August 13th 2014, the Lord called Ruth Home.
To be with Jesus this Earth wasn't her home.
If we want to see her must live by the Book.
We can walk gold streets and sit by the Brook

Living for Jesus is what she did best
We must do it too so in Heaven we'll rest
To live in Eternity with Jesus our Lord
That's when we receive the greatest reward.

Tina Renee Storer

Tina was Marge's niece, whom she dearly loved.

Forty-nine years is not very long,
For a child to live that did no wrong.
We thank God for the years we had,
With this blue-eyed Angel, but God we're sad.

Taken away in the twinkling of an eye,
We don't understand, God why?
We know you have the last say,
We're praying we'll see her again someday.

No more broken bones or sickness to bare,
Many a cast little Tina did wear.
She was in pain a lot of the time,
But kept on going like she was fine.

Little David will remind us everyday,
That Tina still lives in him some way.
She will always be in our mind and heart.
This precious child will live in our heart. Always.

Darrell Glenn Ross

Darrell was Marge's nephew, whom she loved.

Fifty-four years is a very short time,
To be taken away, leaving family and wife.
He loved to play and he loved to live,
Helping others, he loved to give.

Motorcycles and guns were his delight.
He worked at day and played at night.
He was a master mind, could do anything,
Intelligent man, worked on everything.

We don't understand why he suffered so long,
But God had a reason, He took Darrell Home.
Leaving a void in our hearts today,
If we live for Jesus, we'll see him someday.

New Family

I inherited a new family,
The Boughton's and Brooks.
They all are blondes,
They have good looks.

Now Abigail is family,
So we add one more.
I love my new family,
I couldn't love them more.

Marily and Joe are good as gold,
I'll live with them, my home I sold.
Christie loves it here, watches animals play.
Squirrels and chipmunks, they play every day.

The Watermelon

The funniest thing I've ever seen,
Happened in the back seat of our limousine.
This big watermelon, Daddy had bought,
Jumped off the seat and did a somersault.

We drove through the field in our Model A car,
Headed for the spring that wasn't very far.
Too cool, that melon, for us Greene's to eat.
I thought it was all over when it jumped off the seat.

I laughed until my sides were sore,
I cried a while then laughed some more,
The tears rolled down my face like rain,
That jumpin' watermelon was the funniest thing.

On the way home my Daddy said,
"Maggie, You've cried till your face is all red,"
I didn't quit cryin' 'till we got to the house,
Pone was just watchin' me, quiet as a mouse.

Daddy told Mommy, "it jumped off the seat,"
"Goin' to the spring to keep it from the heat,"
"Said I got tickled and laughed 'till I cried,"
"I'll never forget that watermelon's ride."

Brown Bowl

To my daughter, Marilyn Sue.

All my life I've had a little bowl.
The story touches my inner soul.
I remember it well as a child so small,
Once every month us kids had a ball.

To a Farm Bureau meeting our Daddy would go.
We were poor folks, didn't have much dough.
He always had candy for that special night.
Our bowls filled with candy, what a delight.

Mommy read Bible stories while we ate.
Then Daddy came home pretty late.
We'd all say our prayers and go off to bed.
"Go to sleep children," Mommy and Daddy said.

I think back now and think, "wow,
How'd we ever make it?" I didn't know how.
But God was with us all the way,
That's what you call 'the good ole days.'

How old do you think this little bowl is?
Antique dealer wants it, but it's not his.
Money can't buy it, money never will.
I'll give it to Marilyn for her to fill.

As I pass it on down to my daughter, you see,
She'll treasure it and keep it in remembrance of me.
The story is sweet, I remember it well.
No money can buy it, 'cause I won't sell.

Squirrels In A Jar Feeder

The jars are filled with squirrels galore
Eating their seeds and wanting more
Corn on the cob is almost gone
They have been eating since early dawn.

One squirrel to a jar is all you need
Then fill it full of sunflower seed
One little squirrel with a bobbed off tail
Was saved from a Hawk much to his avail.

That Hawk bit off three inches of his tail
Didn't stop him though he can still sail
Up the tree he went and in a hole
Stayed hid a long time just like a mole.

When he came out he ran like mad
If the Hawk had caught him I'd been mad
I fight like a tiger to keep them all fed
When they get filled up they go off to bed.

Folgers Coffee

I wake up in the morning
With Folgers on my mind
You just can't resist it
There is no other kind.

Hot coffee in the morning
Hot coffee all day long
Folgers is the best there is
Make it weak or make it strong.

You will never want any of the rest
Once you have had Folgers best.

Red Lobster

Red Lobster, Red Lobster, don't close your door.
I love your shrimp and so much more.
Coconut sauce is a very good dip.
Once in a while, Frank and I took a trip.

Chillicothe, Ohio was our favorite town.
We'd buy a few things and then shop around.
Then it would be time for us to eat,
Coconut shrimp, it can't be beat.

Bring the little biscuits if they're done.
They sure are good, I can't eat just one.
A baked potato with sour cream galore.
Red Lobster, Red Lobster, don't close your door!

Shopping

Of all the places we like to shop
The store is not far, just a skip and a hop.
The number one store is TJ Maxx.
When we come out don't count our sacks.

Oh, another one, Marshalls' big store,
They have the clothes and shoes galore.
All kinds of purses with fancy names,
Nothing like shopping, it's all in the game.

When we tally up the things we got,
The bill is higher than we thought.
It's one of those things we love to do,
Use the blue card, then we're through.

Dan The Man

Dan The Man works as hard as he can,
Working in his jewelry store.
He sells the best and sells for less,
And wants you to buy some more.

I did just that, I bought two rings,
Now I don't really need anymore.
He's working on sizing my two,
I'll be through and out the door.

Dan The Man run as fast as you can,
If a man comes in with a gun.
Now if you have a gun, put him on the run,
And know your money, he got none.

Richie

AKA Haystack

Muffler Bros. depend on Richie each day
To run some errands, they can't get away.
He will run to the bank, pick up a snack
And before you know it, he's right back.

Sometimes he bakes and takes food galore.
If that's not enough, he makes some more.
He's a very good cook, the best I've known
He takes them things from the garden he's grown.

Patty enjoys everything that he cooks.
He doesn't need Betty Crocker cookbooks.
After that, he gets a coconut pie,
He might eat it all, that makes me cry.

If You Can't Sleep

You go to bed to go to sleep,
If you can't sleep, count some sheep.
If you don't count the sheep, get out of bed,
Say your prayers and go back to bed.

If you're still awake, go get a treat,
Pretzels or corn puffs can't be beat.
That will help you, go back to bed.
Don't tell anyone what I just said.

I'm Too Old To Cry Anymore

Oh, the things I've gone through,
Never seemed to bother you,
But I worked until my feet were sore,
I won't care anymore,
If you walk out that door,
I'm too old to cry anymore.

No more tears will hit the floor,
I'll be happy once more,
Life will go on for me,
Things will be different than before,
When you walk out that door,
I'm too old to cry anymore.

I won't cry anymore,
I'll have new friends galore,
It's something we have to do,
It's so, very, very sad,
We can't be friends anymore,
I'm too old to cry anymore.

Chorus:

Too old to cry or even try,
I did my best for you for years,
Don't call me anymore,
I have opened a new door,
I'm too old to cry anymore.

Candlelite

I've worked many places and I had a lot of fun,
Candlelite was the best and we got our work done.
We worked hard and we worked in the heat,
But old Candlelite was a factory hard to beat.

Not much time for lunch so we ate in.
We'd eat big tomatoes Lisa brought in.
Gracie had a garden, big tomatoes galore.
I really never saw any that big before.

After lunch, back to work, candles everywhere.
Falling off the belt, but we didn't care.
It's running too fast, slow this thing down.
Bosses never see it, they're nowhere around.

When I changed departments, the stockroom you see,
I liked it much better, it was easier on me.
I loved third shift, I was really my own boss.
I did my best so they wouldn't take a loss.

Let's Strive To Keep The Drunks Off Our Nation's Highway

In this great big land of freedom that we call U.S.A.
We take our lives for granted but it could end just any day
Nothing seems important till tragedy comes along
Lets all work together with the words of this song.

When your friends are on the bottle
PLEASE don't let them drive
We must keep our children and families alive
Let's strive to keep the drunk off our nation's highway
Let's turn back to GOD and just pray, pray, pray.

Keep praying to GOD He will pull us through
No matter what our problem GOD is always true
We're MAD about the laws that are broken every day
Let's turn back to GOD and just pray, pray, pray.

Adults and little children are the victims of this crime
We must pull together and make the drunkard do his time
GOD gives us the word to live by everyday
Let's turn back to GOD and just pray, pray, pray.

Chorus:

Let's turn back to GOD, He'll turn this world around
Our burdens He will bare if we lay them down
Let's take it to GOD, He who understands
Take it to the altar, leave it in GOD'S hands.

Ohio Press Release:

Gospel songwriter Marge Keaton was inspired to write, "Let's Strive To Keep The Drunks Off Our Nation's Highway" when told such a song could help save lives and prevent injuries. It is her hope that the song will inspire Christian women across America to join with the Women's Christian Temperance Union to renew a war against the abuse of alcohol.

"This will be a victory for Jesus," she said from her Ohio home. "It is for His glory that we must unite to keep drunk drivers away from our loved ones." Marge is the author of numerous songs that have been recorded.

A Cold Ohio Winter

On a cold, winter night, the snow blowing hard,
It was making big snow drifts out in the yard.
The temp is down to two and I'm down with the flu,
Lord, what in the world am I gonna do?

It's been cold for thirty days, and thirty days it has snowed,
It's been the worst Winter I have ever known.
Cars stalled here and there gotta jump 'em so they'll run.
I tell you, this cold weather isn't any fun.

You take way down south where it's eighty-eight degrees,
The warm winds a blowin' through the palm trees.
They're laying on the beach getting golden tan,
Writing notes to their lovers in the white sand.

But up here in the north, the roads slick with ice,
When you live in Ohio, you pay the price.
They say spring's around the corner, what corner do you mean?
It's been the coldest winter that I have ever seen.

Summer Vacation 1985

Two weeks from the job, vacation's begun,
My daughter to see in the Florida sun.
I'll lay on the dock, 'till I'm brown as a bear,
One night my Marily will frost my hair.

A surprise for me, was her brand new boat,
Something I hadn't expected, it sure got my goat.
We had lots of fun on the Fourth of July,
Watching fireworks, high in the sky.

From out in the ocean, anchored at sea,
The water glistened like a lighted marquee.
Going back home, walking the boat part way,
Are things you remember, tide gets low in the bay.

We went shelling and shopping and ate at the best,
They made me feel like, I was an honored guest.
Soon the good times were over, back to the rat race,
Work is waiting at home, and so is my Pace.

Fourth of July 2024

July Fourth twenty twenty four,
A lot hotter than the day before.
Much too hot to grill them dogs,
Take them off the fire and cool them logs.

On The Beach

Marily and Joe are on the beach,
We just talked they're easy to reach.
Umbrella keeping her cool as it can,
She'll come home with a gorgeous tan.

Miss Elena

In the heat of August, down the Florida coast,
Came a tropical storm to say the most.
Ten counties wide, the folks moved out,
Everything in it's path was tossed about.

Miss Elena wasn't welcome at all,
When she was supposed to hit, she began to stall.
'Take a turn for the west,' the families prayed,
While folks along the coast in shelter stayed.

After three long days and sleepless nights,
A little relief came into sight.
She headed for the west and a different post,
Elena went wild, just a 'rippin' the coast.

Number five for the season, she's the worst one yet,
She left people homeless and thousands in debt,
But my children were spared, I'm thankful to say,
I'll give the Lord praises everyday.

Chorus:

You hurricanes are a terrible sight,
Leavin' people homeless in the night,
We're glad this one's gone away to stay,
Don't ever come ashore, stay out in the bay.

Going On Seventy-Three

Don't get angry with me if I'm slow to speak,
I'm getting older, sometimes I'm weak.
I remember back when I was pretty fast,
Years ago now in the past.

I'll do my best to keep moving about,
I'd like to stay healthy, strong, and stout.
But if I can't, don't get upset with me,
Right now I'm going on seventy three.

I got aches and pains like all the rest,
I'm not always at my very best.
I'll keep going as long as I can,
Keep holding on to God's big hand.

If I can't keep up, you go ahead,
I'll be behind you cause I'm not dead.
Just slower than I used to be,
Don't forget, I'm nearly seventy three.

I plan on 100 if the Lord don't come,
Some people think that's pretty dumb.
I want to live on my own till that last day,
In my own home I want to stay.

I'll live by myself there is no doubt,
Always be able to get about.
If I am slower than I used to be,
Check my birthday, I'm nearly seventy three.

I Found My Pet

God knew I needed some company,
I wanted a little cat to snuggle with me.
We donated some food at our vet,
And what do you know, there was my pet.

This nice Dr. Joe wouldn't take any pay,
We were not prepared for a cat that day.
But we got ready, brought her home.
Now she has a forever home.

Marily and I love her with all our heart,
Can't ever think about being apart.
She likes to sleep on my chest,
She gets settled in for a good night's rest.

Little Christie

I fell in love with Christie at Dr. Joe's.
I wanted another cat, everyone knows.
I love black and white, she's marked so well.
We love each other, as everyone can tell.

She helped me through the bad times and cuddles with me.
Little Christie, I sure love you and she loves me.
She stays close to me or on my chest.
That's the way we go to sleep and get our rest.

I Love You Christie

I love you, little Christie, I like to hold you tight.
I love when you pet me with your paws of white.
I love you, little Christie, when you cuddle with me.
You're the best little baby I ever did see.

I put you in your stroller to go see the birds,
Can't tell you how you have helped me, can't put it into words.
I'll fasten the top down to keep you inside,
Then take you on a ride to explore the outside.

We'll watch all the birds and wonder why,
They fly all around and fly so high.
They make their nest high up in the tree,
God made all kinds for us to see.

Christie Ann

My baby girl is Christie Ann.
I named her after Nanny Ann.
Cant leave her long, I miss her so.
Now I can take her wherever I go.

She's a support animal, got papers and all.
I can take her everywhere, even the mall.
I hate to leave her, 'cause we both cry.
Even if I hold her and kiss her goodbye.

So I'll put her in the stroller and ride her around.
I can take her everywhere, even downtown.
So I'll sit on the patio and watch for deer.
Christie watches for birds, there's plenty out here.

Christie Baby

I love my baby, she means so much to me.
She loves to cuddle and sleep next to me.
She sleeps on my legs and on my back.
Gives me a massage, I like it like that.

I believe the Lord saved her just for me.
He knew I needed some company.
My first look at her, my heart skipped a beat.
I knew it was meant for us to meet.

So I took her home, she's so good for me.
When I feel bad, she comforts me.
Christie Ann is her new name,
I'll bet Dr. Joe was glad I came.

Christie

Christie, Christie, you're gonna be bald,
Your hair is coming out like you got scald.
What will I do with a hairless cat?
Guess I'll buy you a coat and a fur hat.

Kitty Talk

I'm lonesome tonight, old memories come back.
Keeps me a thinkin' about this and that.
No one to talk to but Christie, my cat.
I could talk all night but she can't talk back.

I'm teaching her to talk, today I heard a new word.
It's different from anything I ever heard.
I'm learning new words everyday,
Then she teaches me in her kitty way.

I try to understand, with her little voice,
She don't talk loud, don't make much noise.
I could listen all night to no avail.
But I understand by the swishing of her tail.

Tommy Keaton

Poor little Tommy was left alone,
Someone dumped him out at our home.
He was black as coal, but had white feet.
He was so hungry, I got him something to eat.

He played in the yard, loved climbing trees.
I said you're scaring my birds, come down please.
So we went out front to the cherry tree,
He would climb, turn upside down, and look up at me.

He would chase me around, then tackle me.
I'd be feeding the deer, he'd hang onto me.
It was so cold in the garage at night,
Leaving him in there just wasn't right.

Seventeen below was too cold in his bed,
You're coming in tonight, that's what I said.
With Frank in the hospital, I was alone.
So I brought him in, he loved his warm home.

Tommy

I loved my Tommy, he was my first cat
He was so healthy, some thought he was fat
He was my companion after all I went through
He was good medicine for when I was blue.

We played hide and seek, first he'd hide from me
Then I hid from him and he'd come looking for me.
The good times we had, I'll never forget
I tell you the truth, he was my best pet.

He was fourteen years old, he was feeling very bad
It hurt to see him suffer, he felt so bad
We had a long talk, I looked in his eyes
We thought it was time to go to paradise.

It left my home empty, I couldn't hardly stay
No one was here, Marily and Joe gone away
They were gone three weeks, the beach they did roam
So I was here alone 'till they came home.

Kandi Christmas

I loved you, Kandi, with all my heart,
When you left, you took a piece of my heart.
I'll never forget the cute things you done,
The first day I saw you, my heart you won.

The things you brought and layed at my feet,
Like the rack of ribs, yeah, I let you eat,
'Cause I saw big brown eyes looking back at me,
They're all yours, don't give them to me.

You brought me a dollar, layed it at my feet,
Got it from somewhere down the street.
Any other name wouldn't fit, you were so sweet.
Kandi was perfect with your four white feet.

Your hair was beautiful, brown, black, and tan.
I loved to brush you as much as I can.
I'd cut it for summer to keep you cool,
We even bought you a swimming pool.

Now you're in Heaven, have you seen Nikki yet?
She's up there I know, God loves a good pet.
Look for Chynna, Aja, Pierre and Pacey too,
I can't wait to see y'all, your health brand new.

Mama Bird

Mama bird is raising a family again,
Sitting on four eggs, she's a little "wren."
A hawk got her other babies, she's trying again,
I wish he'd go back to where he'd been.

He waited 'till they were ready to fly,
He darted down from high in the sky.
I hope they hurry, get out of his way,
So he has to look elsewhere for his prey.

From The Heart Of Marge

I love you Honey.

I wondered many times what would I do
If you went to Heaven before I do
Can I stay here in our home alone
With all the memories and friends we've known.

No one knows how hard you worked
To make this house a home
I want to stay as long as I can
My lord my Savior will help me along.

Frank I have loved you for 24 years
There's been heartaches and sorrow, shed some tears.
The happy and good times outweigh the bad
You are Marilyn's best Dad she ever had.

Frank, you have been so good to Marilyn and me,
You fought for us and our country.
You fought a good fight and came home safe,
No one else could take your place.

Rocky Fork Lake Home

Rocky Fork Lake, in Ohio, was added to
the State Park System in 1950

Our old home shows wear and tear,
As I reminisce about things up there.
We had good times at the lake.
I'd like to go back, for old-time sake.

The beautiful Dam is on the east side,
A beautiful sight from a boat ride.
Thirty-one miles of shoreline,
The road goes past the old home of mine.

I've been under the water floor,
All that dirt and mud galore.
We drove down in and all about,
In nineteen fifty they were digging it out.

Two thousand eighty acres is what they made,
You can sunbathe, fish, or sit in the shade.
I have a lot of memories of the beautiful lake.
Yes, I'd like to go back for old-time sake.

The Day I Met Frank Keaton

I said no, no, no, I won't get married again,
But Jesus knew best, He knows all about men.
This man at our church had lost his wife,
And John Wright thought he needed another wife.

I barely knew him, we never did meet.
Wright said let's all four go somewhere to eat.
Chillicothe was our town, Red Lobster's where we ate
Then we headed for our homes before it got too late.

The more we were together, the happier we became.
So we started making plans to change my last name.
Frank set the date for the ninth of May
Nineteen ninety-eight was our Wedding Day.

I became his wife we were happy as could be.
We did everything together we were one you see.
Then tragedy came along it took my love away,
But I'll see him again on that Homecoming Day.

Written for our 26th Anniversary May 9th 2024

Frank & Marge

One of the happiest days of my life
Was when I married Frank, the love of my life.
We were married almost twenty-four years,
Now he is gone, my eyes full of tears.

I'm trying to mend my broken heart.
Don't know what to do, don't know where to start.
But I will make it one day at a time,
Jesus is with me so it will be fine.

He will take me home when my time is up.
We'll sit at His table with Him we will sup.
My name's on my mansion welcomes me home,
Forever to live in that Heavenly Home.

Then I'll be with Frank the rest of my life,
Where there's no worries, heartache or strife.
We all have loved ones gone on before,
Then we'll be with them forever more.

Frank has entered the white Pearly Gates,
He was ready to go, he had no wait.
He was welcomed in, I've read the good book,
All the Earthly things he never took.

We have to go alone, it's the Master's Plan,
He will greet us hand in hand.
Frank's name was written in the Lamb's Book of Life.
He will live there, the rest of his life.

Marge and Frank Keaton

Our Wedding Day

May 9, 1998

Frankie I sure miss you,
I'm lonesome tonight.
If only you were with me,
I'd hold you so tight.

Our church was our life,
We enjoyed it so much.
All the things that we did,
And the hearts that were touched.

We had laughter and fun
As we went on our way.
One thing so special
Our Wedding Day.

Frankie

I'll never get over losing you,
I just don't know what to do.
I can't be myself without you,
I'm just lost, Frankie, without you.

Soon I'll be in that Holy Place,
I'll get to hug you, see your smiling face.
I'll tell you how much I have missed you.
It was special, our love that we knew.

Soon, I'll be in your arms again.
You won't have to say "I'll never leave you again."
We'll be together with Jesus I know.
My King James Bible tells me so.

Frankie Your Memories Live On

You're in Heaven with Jesus I know.

If I could hold you in my arms one more time,
Maybe it would satisfy my mind.
I have missed you so, no one will ever know.
Your memories are vivid in my mind.

Sometimes there are things I'd like to ask you,
I just wish we'd had more time.
God saw you in so much pain,
He took you Home with Him to rein.

Memories Frank

I'd like to be in Frank's arms again
And hear him say, "I'll never leave you again."
We'll be together over there and never part
You know I loved him with all my heart.
"I'd like to be in Frank's arms again."

Twenty four years was not long enough,
Because we loved each other so much.
We told each other every night,
How much we loved then kissed goodnight.
"I'd like to be in Frank's arms again."

I'm homesick to see Frank again.
Seems like our lives had just began.
I'll see him soon I cannot wait,
Until I enter the White Pearly Gates.
"I want to be in Frank's arms again."

Frank

I've cried a river of tears over you.
I did it because I really loved you.
I thought I had loved but it wasn't true
I never really loved anyone but you.

Today it will be twenty six years.
I'm thinking about you, holding back the tears.
The good times we had outweigh the bad.
You were the best husband anyone could have.

Memories of Frank

Sometimes I think I'll lose my mind,
I never thought you would leave me behind.
Sometimes I can hear you call my name,
I answer but its all in vain.

Sometimes I wake up thinking of you,
I have to start my day without you.
Your memories never go away,
I'll be with you again someday.

Sometimes I can see you in your chair,
I think, "you know, life isn't fair."
I hear your voice in my ears,
Saying, "Marge I love you," it always brings tears.

Feeling Sad

As I sit here tonight, I don't know what to do.
All the heartache and sorrow I've been through.
I've lost so much, all in one year,
No wonder I cried a river of tears.

I have no one to talk to but Christie my cat.
She understands me but she can't talk back.
Marily comes down, but she has so much to do.
She works all day, but never gets through.

I Had To Let Him Go

Frank Keaton was the love of my life.
He's living with Jesus the rest of his life.
No one knows how I miss him so,
He suffered so much, I had to let him go.

He can see good now, he has no pain.
He walks just perfect, without his cane.
Heaven gained an angel, this I know.
I kissed him goodbye, I had to let him go.

But someday if we live for God,
This old Earth we'll never more trod.
We'll be together in our Heavenly home
This old Earth is not our home.

I'll see him again by the Crystal Sea.
I'll be there soon, he said he'd wait for me.
We can all go if we live right,
Jesus will walk with us day and night

He was the best father, Marilyn ever had.
She loved him dearly, she called him Dad.
Dad loved her with all his heart,
He missed her so much when they were apart.

"Call Marily," he'd say, to pray for me,
I know she will 'cause she loves me.
She drove up, didn't drive slow,
We had good times together, but we had to let him go.

Moved to Georgia

I left my home at Rocky Fork Lake,
Had to hurry and pack, didn't know what to take.
After losing Frank, I couldn't think straight.
It was our plan to go, it wasn't a mistake.

So I went to Georgia with Marily you see,
That's where Frank said he wanted me to be.
Too much on me to care for our home,
It wouldn't be safe for me to be alone.

I left a lot of things and memories behind,
Like my neighbors and friends that were so kind.
It's twelve months today since I moved here,
It's hard to believe it's been a year.

Marily and Joe are so good to me,
No other place that I'd want to be.
I like the weather it's warmer here,
Time has gone fast this last year.